FAMILY ROOM

Damon Young

Family Room

© Damon Young

First Edition 2020

ISBN: 978-1-913329-19-8

Published by Dempsey & Windle
15 Rosetrees
Guildford
Surrey
GU1 2HS
UK
01483 571164
dempseyandwindle.com

British Library Cataloguing-in-Publication Data

A catalogue record for this book is available from the British Library

For Lorca Ramone Young

Acknowledgements

'Proud Feet' first appeared in the Dempsey and Windle anthology *What the Peacock Replied* (2019).

'Thomas Bew's Armistice' was shortlisted for the Wells Festival of Literature Prize, 2019.

'Contact' was shortlisted for The Robert Graves Poetry Prize, 2018 and longlisted for the Canterbury Festival Poet of the Year Prize, 2019.

'Hotel- Family Room' first appeared in *Reach Poetry*.

'Patting Your Pockets' first appeared in *Dream Catcher Magazine*.

'Boxer' first appeared in *Marble Poetry*.

'Pride' first appeared in *Reach Poetry*.

'7 Dane Road' first appeared in *Reach Poetry*.

'She Told Me' first appeared in *The University of Reading Creative Arts Anthology* (2019).

'Rice Paper' was winner of the Alzheimer's Society Poetry Prize, 2019.

'Trial by Combat' first appeared on *Riverside,* the blog of Two Rivers Press.

'Mortality Salience' first appeared in the Dempsey and Windle anthology *What the Moon was Told* (2018).

'Divination' first appeared in *Reach Poetry*.

With thanks for helping me in developing these poems to my fellow poets of the Reading Stanza of the Poetry Society and Thin Raft, in particular Claire Dyer and Gill Learner. Thanks also to Alexandra Butler, Lizzy Rippon and Sue Young for their help and support.

CONTENTS

Proud Feet

Come on Angel-Tiger, kick your proud feet into
your proud boots and let's rub clouds from the sky.

Maybe not those big, lumpy sun shields,
but we can handle those whiskers and wisps.

We will giggle like we are tickled as
they disappear under our thumb whorls;

one eye closed each and mouths twisted in concentration,
as we return our chosen square of sky to blue.

Eat your cinnamon swirls like they are your
school week; thump-jaw every buttery bite

and let me wipe away the persistent,
stray crumbs that stick to your weekend face.

Drag me to the trampoline and bounce poison
out through your toes. Let me tense and gulp

at every prospective bruise, whilst you throw out
your legs at the world rising and falling under your socks.

Thomas Bew's Armistice

My great-great-uncle Thomas Bew foretold his death.
In a poem sent home to mother, he wrote of the mounds
of clay that served as graves across the fields of Flanders:
of angelic voices that rose from that earth and carried loving
words to mothers lost in deep grey pockets of grief.

Yet, in 1918, his voice was within his torn body as
he was ferried, still pulsing, back to his mother's care.
I picture him on Armistice Day, a window cracked open
to skin-pricking November air, bells finding the corners
of his room above sheets stained to the colour of rust.

As peace dropped like blossom, his body remained a battlefield:
a quagmire of white blood cells and sepsis, wounds infected by
the Flanders clay at the moment of their infliction. As life
and rhythm returned to the town's arteries, he died amidst the rebirth:
he and Rhoda Bew, drops in a wave of loss that outlasted the silence of guns.

Contact

She is an elderly woman with blood-spotted lungs;
full of suspicion and self-appointed scrutiny
and is wrenching at my daughter,
who is clinging to me
and I am wearing catastrophe under my skin.

The miracle of my daughter's fingers whiten against
a heartbeat that has always made sense
and she explodes at the bewilderment
of re-found togetherness being torn away.

My daughter's face and body are made for laughter and tantrum;
these screeches and convulsions are from somewhere new.
She screams, 'I want to stay with daddy,'
and, 'I don't want to go to the new house.'
The woman hisses, 'I think you'd better go.'

I move away, look back and see my daughter
in defiant frenzy, twisting to be away from
the skin and bone arms that can barely
contain her, as she tries to get to me, on the humdrum street.

If only she could burst from the helpless sweetness
of her skin and monstrously steeple the road.
If she could shape the warrior twitching in her child-limbs,
she would swat this woman away,
hold me and never be made to let go.

Hotel – Family Room

It beckons, a Roman purple airlock,
the diving bell in which we sink into
deep sea tiredness, having borne the shock
of exfoliating air that whip-blew

us round our wild ride at the city's heights.
You run through these corridors like you
run nowhere else. Elbows wide with delight
and gorgeous flump toes pushing you through

the mossy carpet, peeling off the long
tentacles of the term as you go.
Surfacing shall launch the lifelong
adventures that are planned for tomorrow.

Here we leave separation's hinterland,
arms looped across twin beds, your hand in my hand.

7 Dane Road

Many times now, our shoulders have uncurled
against the soft down and sweet and sour air
of our green and cream sanctuary by the white-spined sea.

From its cracked stone steps we spill like twin puddles
and splash each other down gull-echoing slopes
where we salt-crust our lashes and cascade towards the shore.

Until, sticky-faced, air-dried and exhausted,
you are shoulder carried up lactic hills
to take your place amongst delightful, cosy clutter.

Inside thick walls we ooze into softest rest,
shutters between us and the dog- slick street
as we soak ourselves in connection renewed.

Patting Your Pockets

Patting your pockets with an officious
politeness you would have admired,
was the last time I touched you;
following an enquiry as to whether
personal artefacts were about you.

I had no idea what was about you.
I was beside your stillness. A stillness like
Nannie and Grandad's house when they
were on holiday: their house devoid
of laughter and pre-feast steam was a shell.

I would wait for its reanimation by
sticky plastic and sharp-strawed gifts,
a slideshow of mahogany skin
and places with greenhouse air:
now the empty house of you was lying there.

My hands were much too tentative and soft
to give purpose to my task
and my efforts felt inconsequential
and blurred; I wanted to touch you
and felt that I needed a reason

to steer me decently through the reality
of being alongside the shell of you.
I had held your warm, blood-coursed hand
when I had left that afternoon
and I hoped that living touch had said

what I wanted it to say, as my hands skimmed
the outside of your pockets and paramedics
looked politely and sombrely on.
My task was a shadow motive,
focusing the struggle against feeling you gone.

'Boxer'

For months I had striven for a bodily
articulacy that was just beyond me.
Sometimes there were flashes of long armed
dominance and exaltation in the savage ballet:
a oneness with the flesh that I live in.

I sought an acceptance amongst these men
with Swarfega hands, faith in their reserves of meanness
and loose-limbed grace. I stood amongst
the faces and voices of my childhood
and aspired to the liberating emptiness of violence.

In a training room full of vapour, sweat and muscle;
on a playground-soft floor, I battled the impossibility
of forming a left hook, whilst protecting
my nose and my ego. I once found the
mechanics of unfurling a big right hand

that rhapsodised against my sparring partner's chin.
It sent his face to ten to four. I roared inside
as my shoulders rolled, feigning nonchalance
at my powerful ease. My success disguising
lolloping feet and head and body without twitch or flex.

As the real fight approached, I looked and felt
enough like a fighter to invite those who
had threatened to glimpse me in that way.
Under fierce lights and amongst diffusions of cheap lager,
in the galleon creek of the ring

the charge of his gloved fist pulsed
against my face. His corner-men howled.
I treacle-stepped my way through three rounds
of forest-fire, until my opponent's hand was raised
and we sat silently together in the medical room.

Afterwards and alone, all energy
had been expended. I lay scallop-soft against
scratchy, fibrous carpet, unable to move.
I wanted to hide, but I needed my friends to tell me
that my fraud had not been completely revealed.

Pride

She finds me as I arrive to join her
in a field of celebration and noise.
Her colour drains. I ask, 'Are you alright?'

My mother doesn't answer, so I ask again.
Nothing. Puzzled, with panic rising, I ask once again.
And then I catch the dead weight of her frame;

not a crashing tumble, but a staggered
crumble, a fold, that I shepherd to the
parched and cracked, brown ground.

A drag queen, with curling nightclub lashes
abandons dameish frivolity to be the first at our side.
She looms over us in her huge heels and then

dashes to a water station and returns holding
bottles delivered with urgency and kindness,
concern visible through her pore-deep make-up.

As my mother reaches for her senses,
I think this is it, this is how she goes,
on a smothered September day,

as a drag queen samaritans and rainbow flags
flutter and a Shirley Bassey impersonator
foghorns 'Goldfinger' towards the river.

But her colour returns as she tells me
of how she gleefully joined the march round
town, in the blistering sun, drinking only cider,

eating nothing but chips. Our customary
roles reverse as I eyeroll at her recklessness,
while admiring her verve as we sit and soak up the shade.

Marble

I was outside of the junior school hegemony, skirting the fringes of the pale grey
concrete ground. I spotted someone even further from the whirling centre;
a familiar figure to me, awkward in shorts, with no fixed point to grab in this swirl.

We had shared an infant class and I recalled the Germanic mother, the demanding
younger sister and the party with icing crusted cake. His face seemed overgrown
for his eight years and his intellect too vast for the drab confines of this place.

He had been whisked from my class, his progress accelerated by a year in an
attempt to find a point from which he could project the spectrum of his mind.
Now, here he was and he glowed at the prospect of company.

He had a small marble in his hand, glass with a twirling turquoise streak inside;
playground currency of the lowest value, but currency nonetheless.
We set about our school's version of the game which utilised a manhole cover,

the dips underneath the handles forming the curve of a target, like the pocket
of a pool table. A tanned and scabbed playground veteran
was our first spectator, 'Where's the other marble?' he asked

as school decorum (of which I was ignorant and had not complied) demanded
that each player staked a similar prize and that the winner took all. Our inexpert thumb
thwacks saw the single marble clank randomly against the raised ridges of metal.

I somehow found the balance of force and delicacy required
to twang it home and claim victory. I scooped and pocketed
my reward and rejoined the lunchtime throng without a backward glance.

She Told Me

She told me once, that each time
she heard 'Here Comes the Sun'
she thought of a Praying Mantis:
due to a picture on a classroom wall
and a teacher with a record player.

I was delighted by her easy charm
and the promise of a mind that
worked the same way as mine.
As she strummed her guitar and
laughed, I never questioned what
happened to the fathers of her sons.

Rice Paper

When I was about seven, my mum and I discovered
the novelty of biting through rice paper and letting

it snowflake on our tongues. It was our exotic secret,
pasted fish-skin thin onto a pulpy, seed- ridged fruit bar.

My nan joined us once and we formed a street coven to
sample these strange, freshly bought treats. Mum and I

mischievously withheld our knowledge of the miraculous
edible wrapper and nan's wise, steel-sprung fingers padded

ineffectively at the vacuum-shrunk white
cover. Her face peering at their failure.

My delight at being the bearer of a hidden truth gave way
to the bodily buzz of loss. Those life-coarsened fingers that

seemed to have ripped a place in the world for me, were now
diligent but outfoxed; reduced to the cluelessness of childhood.

Her last days, decades later, seemed a slow erosion back
to the earth from which she was shaped. There was a wildness

beneath her tumbleweed hair and feeding, soothing
and tending became dependent on the hands of others.

A love-beam of a greeting was late to disappear, but eventually
gave way to a frown of alarm, as my shape in the doorway

became unfamiliar to her. Her fingers, stripped of certainty,
became swollen and her gold wedding band began to bite.

Pliers held with surgical care snipped it in two, in
order to relieve its unsustainable pressure. As I looked

at the waxy white circle of newly uncovered skin where
the ring had been, I felt rice paper sadness once more.

I notice a gentle burble of water

creeping down like a sly urine stream,
streaking the plaster as it softly pulses towards the carpet.
The pad of my index finger presses for the source
and feels it, soft as a baby's mouth.
Dynamic action to avoid disaster is not required,
but the inviolate calm of my house is disturbed.

This razor tooth, needle eye puncture
carries none of the devastation of opening
the door onto my child's toys scattered
around the rooms from which she was plucked.
That was a primordial aloneness
suffered in dust dancing stillness.

These days, the boundaries between bedrooms
are morphically blurred, with exhortations to stay
or bedtime story slides into refluxive unconsciousness.
Sometimes on such nights, my growling slumber
is stirred by the playground weight of a heel finding
the dip between my hip and my rib and resting there;
a silent prayer to togetherness.

Panther

I once watched a panther,
inured to her own confinement,
turn delighted, muscular somersaults
against the boundaries of her cage.

I watched her soaring through the air,
until she clumped and buzzed the posts and mesh
that interrupted her mischievous, hunter's spring.
She looked like you, in your shimmering dress.

You catch the scent of my tomcat on your fingertips,
the scent of my pillow on your hair,
as you bring your flat-white up to your lips
and make eyes at the barista from your deep-red chair.

There's a panther pacing her trail
between the line of trees and my door.
She's tired, cold and hungry and her feet are full of thorns,
yet she turns somersaults against the fast encroaching dawn.

Trial By Combat – Fry's Island, Reading

In April 1163, a great concourse of people assembled.
The King himself was there. Essex and Monfort were
ferried over to the island , and were bidden to fight out
their quarrel. Let God judge between them!

Royal Berkshire History
David Nash Ford

Water lapped the island's edge
and branches swayed in calm.

On banks across the silver-streaked,
carp-brown water, crowds would swarm
anticipating death as righteous judgement.

A faith was placed in truth and falsehood
travelling through the flesh where two men lived.

Startled crows would fleck the near-sky
as metallic crash of combat played.

The accuser's limbs found ease
in iron confinement and they sprang
heavy-handed blows upon the accused.

Years after disgrace in sinew and muscle,
followed by the ghost-pulse of survival
came years filled with monastic, faceless living.

The man who'd been Henry of Essex would say
a vision of St Edmund the Martyr loomed

between the island and the clouds,
all vitality draining from his limbs.

Reunion at a forty-something funeral

The moment transcends the years apart
and the reserve of grown men: arms
wrapped around middle aged waists,
fingers gripping warm flesh, as we lean
into each other and form a wigwam of grief.

There are wormholes connecting this
moment to nightclub shenanigans and more.
We share crisp-edged memories from as many
years past as will take us to life's last stages.

We've probably dodged this curse of parents
sobbing at our oak-cased feet, yet we survey
the finite with a gulp and jolt back into
the loss that today has served us: clinging to
continuity in the face of brutal change.

Fenella Beach

Unruly seaweed scratches at the underside of clear water
near where Saint Patrick clambered upon this island.

I am endlessly drawn to such tales of the divine,
yet they are bloodless set against these tendrils of mystery;
the air of centuries of lawlessness.

The sea and sky are framed by two perfectly placed
fingers of land. I can feel the slow grind of evolution
beneath my shoulder blades.

Suspended between parable and the depths
of the earth I feel an inscrutable peace.

Mortality Salience

Today for the first time, she wants to discuss death:
telling me she has said to God that she doesn't
want to die and asking me if it will hurt.
I run through the usual tropes about deep old age
and slipping away to benevolent final sleep.

Afterwards, as I watch her rosy fingers spread
across piano keys, her feet dangling above the pedals,
her back set in the perfect posture of childhood,
I am assaulted by the fact that one day she will die
and I will not be there to share it with her,
unless. . .

So, I am forced into hoping that the memory
of this milk-toothed, dance-eyed smile
will be gone long before she goes.

She swings round from her self-discovered arpeggios
and catches the creases of projected grief upon my face.

Within minutes we tumble soft and reckless
through the full range of our games
and the shadow of our fragility is sun-bleached and is gone.

Kissing Achilles

Stretching across ribs, in block black
is Achilles, spear pointing down
towards an exposed throat.

Fingertips trace his outline,
bumping the mole that rises from the shield.
Lips gently exhale, ruffling the fine hairs
of the skin that carries his image.

The lips land and then her face lifts,
scanning the journey taken by her fingers.
Her eyes meet mine and blaze.

Divination

We walk over the wide streets, built on layers of bones;
the plague dead, monarchs, and other fossils of the great ages.

Towering, marble sarcophogi rise over us and centuries of
wealth and its counterpoint are carved into the air.

We step away from the bustle and the plod and find a room
of old, dark oak, now opportuned for coffee and oat milk.

The inside of its panes trickle with generations of damage.

Your voice starts to fade into the bleat of the street,
your skin becomes softer still, waning to translucence.

I can see the blue network of your travelling lifeblood
until it dilutes and dissolves. I try to grab a last chance

to read your entrails, but they give way to
sinew and calcium before everything is gone.

This city now houses your absence. It is where I will remember you.

This is a place

to encase irrepressible sound
and envelop intricate silence,

where draped shapes sleep, awaiting skilful
hands to draw sonorous air from their curves

and intimate stories curl their way
around the hundreds gathered to receive them.

This is a place that is a point of departure,
where inspiration flies on exhaled breath

to escape these walls and
vapour-trail across the stars.